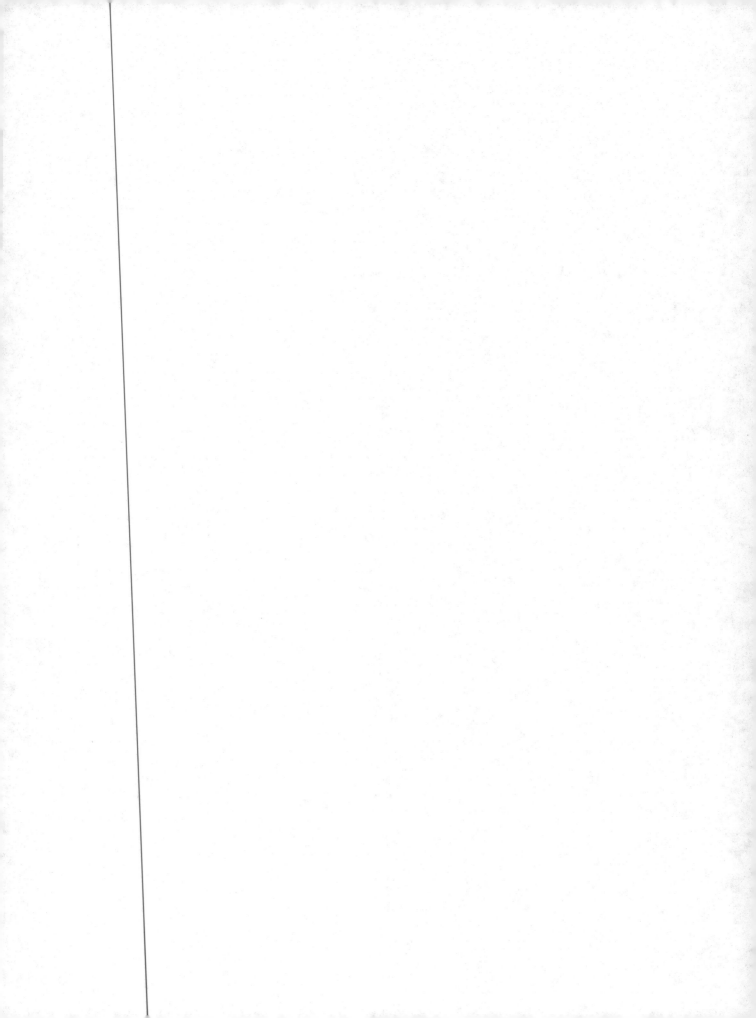

DEDICATION

For Anselm and the memory of the tree that defied the laws of nature.

The subject matter contained in this book is original work reflecting the author's study. It is not meant to be used in place of medical or psychological treatment. Susan Gurnee, the publishers, editors, translators and distributors remain free of any responsibility for the readers' breadth of exploration in the territory of intuition. Be observant. Learn in a leisurely fashion. Celebrate your progress. Use your common sense.

Cover art courtesy of Sue Gurnee.
Chapter heading photography courtesy of Oliver Brenneisen.
Layout design by Ron Tayyab.

Published by AuthorHouse   03/15/2012
ISBN: 978-1-4685-6418-1 (sc)
ISBN: 978-1-4685-6417-4 (e)

Library of Congress Control Number: 2012904873

AuthorHouse™
1663 Liberty Drive
Bloomington, IN 47403
www.authorhouse.com
Phone: 1-800-839-8640

intuition
enhancement
in five simple steps

SUSAN GURNEE

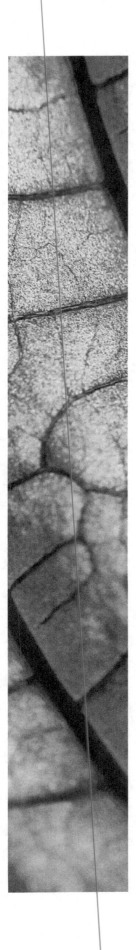

CONTENTS

Introduction   9

Chapter One – Your Five Senses   12

Chapter Two – Five Areas of the Brain   18

Chapter Three – Five Ways to Build Certainty and Trust   28

Chapter Four – Five Ribbons of Reality   34

Chapter Five – Five Finger Flicking - A Technique   40

Bonus Exercises   42

About The Author   47

Glossary   50

INTRODUCTION

This manual is for individuals who have had personal intuitional experiences and want to strengthen their innate gifts. Although you will be involved with a compilation of unproven theories, these time-tested procedures have enriched countless students from a variety of cultural backgrounds and levels of interests.

I continue to research and fine-tune my natural gifts. This began as a personal hobby and segued into a profession. I bent spoons, found lost animals, communicated with race horses, balanced the energy fields of trainers, ballet troupes, movie stars, musicians, artists, government leaders and royalty. My brain was tested in laboratory settings while doing energetic healings and while solving complex puzzles over vast distances. Quietly, from my studio in the woods, I have maintained an international healing practice since 1985.

There is still so much to learn in this vast realm called intuition. I will never tire of its interconnections and synchronicities.

In these chapters you will learn:

1. methods to organize incoming sensory and meta-sensory data

2. a management system for five parts of your brain

3. an energetic support technique to increase intuitional accuracy

4. five ways to trust your intuition as a problem-solving tool

5. pleasure-filled exercises to strengthen your intuitive abilities

Enriching your ability to obtain accurate intuitive answers at a moment's notice is a vital necessity in times of change.

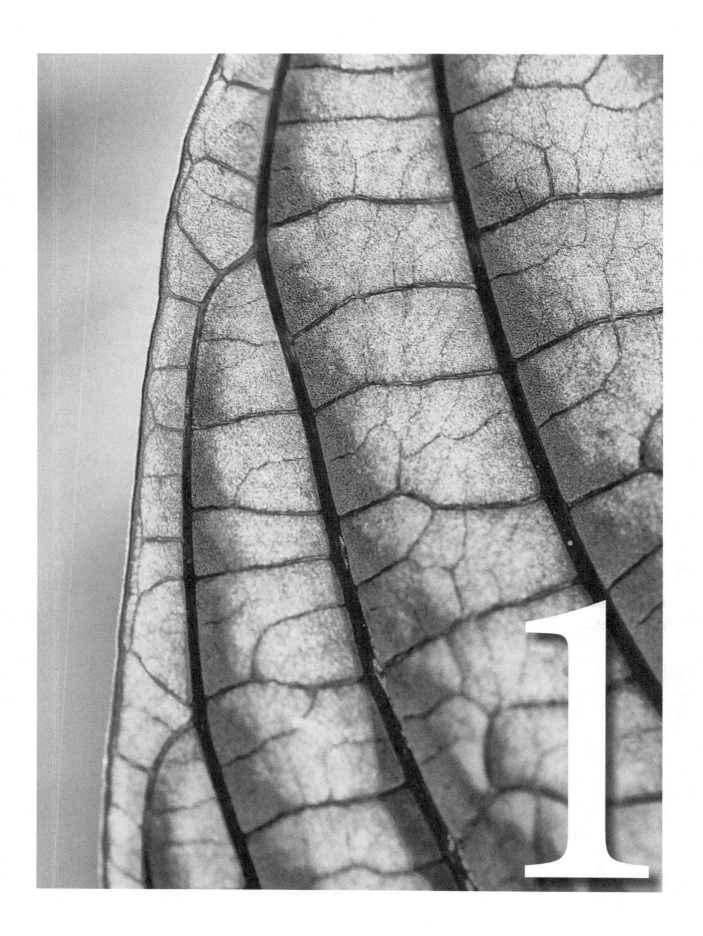

1

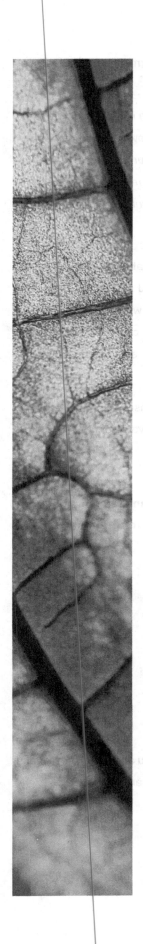

YOUR FIVE SENSES

The goals of this chapter are to focus awareness on incoming sensory information and to practice methods to consciously build easily retrievable files.

You are sitting in a black wrought iron chair eating a ripe tomato slice which is balanced on a warm slab of freshly baked bread. The sun filters through wisteria vines above your head and shadow patterns dance on the warm sunlit stone patio. Clusters of light purple flowers share their scent when the wind blows from the west. Birds and insects alternate their rhythmic melodies sometimes quite near and then just within range of the sunlit mountains.

It is with your five senses that you experience your world.

When you taste a sandwich on a patio in the summer, the focus on the tomato's flavor is called specific. Ambient is the term for peripherally listening to the birds and picking up the environmental details. Specific shows you what - and the ambient tells you where. Specific and ambient information from your five senses filter through a part of your brain called the Reticular Activating System. The information is sent through your Limbic System, the seat of emotions, and processed in your unique way in the hemispheres of your brain.

With just minutes of directed sensory training each day, you can build sensory files that contain extremely detailed specific and ambient information. Orderly files sharpen your connection to each moment. Orderly files strengthen your short and long-term memory.

Orderly sensory files help you discern a wide range of subtleties. Your sensory training prepares you to easily gather meta-sensory details. In a similar manner as remembering the color or texture of an object, you will soon be able to retrieve intuitional details with equal vividness whenever you desire.

Your five senses include:

> **SIGHT**
>
> **HEARING**
>
> **SMELL**
>
> **TASTE**
>
> **TOUCH**

Together, they inform you about your surroundings.

Practice using the following **SENSORY AWARENESS LISTS** to remind you about the specific and ambient information that it is possible to record and retain from the world around you.

SENSORY AWARENESS LIST

SIGHT - vision

Practice expanding the details of what you see using these categories as reference points:

Colors

Light and shadow

Movement

Sizes and relative dimensions

Shapes

HEARING - sound/noise

Practice remembering the variety of sounds you encounter by noticing the specific elements in these categories:

Volume / Location

Dull noise

Sharp sound

High or low pitch

Harmonic / echo

Unidentifiable

When you sense something unfamiliar, take time to find out more about it by switching from the ambient to the specific as you investigate.

Does this sound have any similarity to others you have experienced? Often by association you can learn to distinguish further subtleties.

SMELL – odors/fragrances

Practice noticing the wide variety of odors you encounter and strengthen your memory by placing them into these defined categories:

Sweet

Floral

Burnt

Acrid

Minty

Citrus

Unidentifiable

When you experience an unfamiliar odor, bring your attention only to your sense of smell as you investigate. Check your experiential files.

Can you remember other odors that were similar?

Often people say that some odors have "a chemical smell". How would you redefine this general description so that it includes the mixture of the categories above?

TASTE – flavor/temperature/texture

Practice identifying the flavors you encounter using these categories:

> **Salty**
>
> **Sweet**
>
> **Sour**
>
> **Bitter**
>
> **Astringent**
>
> **Pungent (spicy)**

When you experience an unfamiliar flavor, focus on different parts of your tongue to investigate. The tip of the tongue registers sweet. The two sides of the tongue have receptors for salty and sour. The back of the tongue registers bitterness. The center of the tongue has only a few taste buds but can clearly identify astringent and pungent flavors.

TOUCH – feeling/pressure

Practice placing things you touch into categories by their:

> **Surface texture**
>
> **Temperature**
>
> **Density**
>
> **Solidity**
>
> **Substance**
>
> **Unidentifiable**

When you find something unfamiliar, apply pressure to gain further information. Register both the surface feel as well as the other information into your files.

Practice placing your direct attention on details of the environment that are above and below you as well as to your left and right. Practice moving your head rather than just your eyes to pick up cues. When you do, more than just the automatic activities of the brain are engaged. This way you build new pathways of arousal, orientation and focus.

Recognition of your body's sensations creates your language of sensitivity.

NOTES

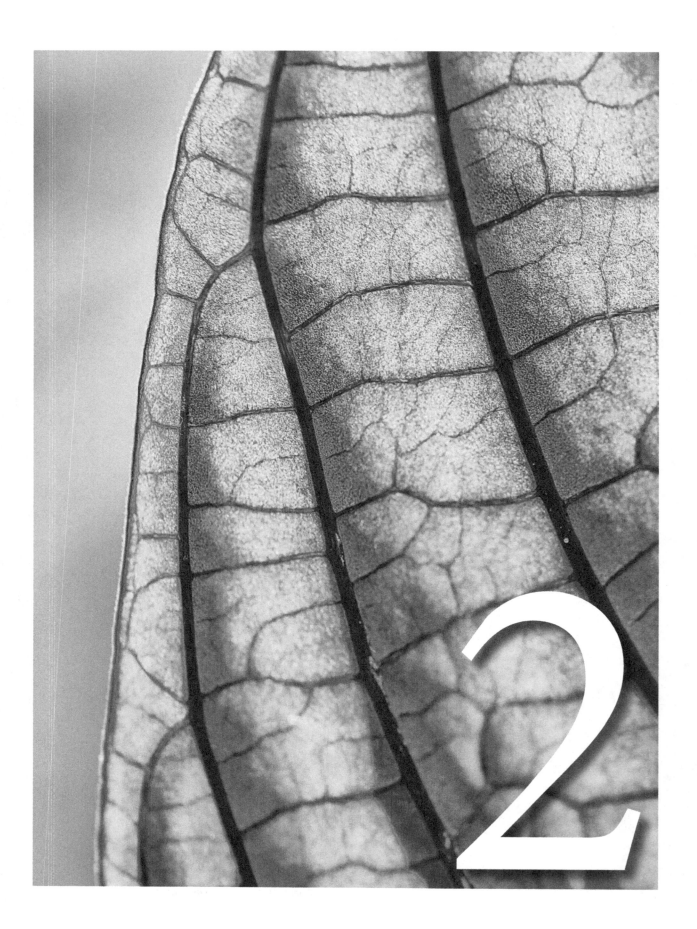

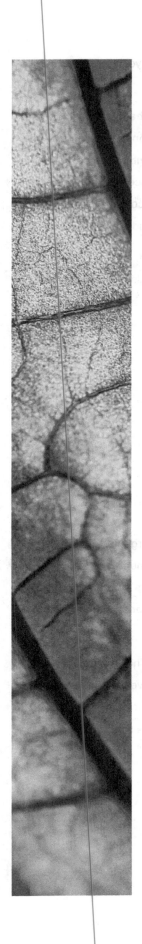

CHAPTER 2
FIVE AREAS OF THE BRAIN

The goal of this chapter is to strengthen the communication channels from your conscious mind to the five impulse-processing parts of your brain.

Imagine that your brain is an ever-changing interconnection of networks that fit neatly together. Sensory input alters these and creates perceptions. Then these perceptions create an altered impact that further alters perceptions. Patterns that linger will connect with other groups of neurons and form associative clusters that create ideas and memories. Since your brain does not see, feel or hear, it is a likened to a construction site of stimuli. This constantly adapting inner environment can be trained to pick up subtle information that is beyond the realm of your five senses.

Once you know your way around your brain, you can use your attention skills to enhance your well-organized circuitry.

The parts of the brain that will be highlighted this chapter include:

1. **Left Hemisphere of your brain**
2. **Right Hemisphere of your brain**
3. **Reticular Activating System**
4. **Limbic System**
5. **Fulgent Cadences**

As a baby grows, a sculpting process called apoptosis occurs. This organizing process of the neurons strengthens a pairing process. If cells do not find their placement, they diminish and die. When telepathy is actively practiced as a form of communication, there is a greater chance for a baby to pair intuition impulses. These, when nurtured can aid intution enhancement in a growing youngster.

Each human has twin hemispheres that are a mirror image of each other. They are held together by fibres that maintain a continuous communication. When information arrives in one hemisphere, it is made available to the other. Then a seemingly single stream of consciousness ensues. Each hemisphere has a distinctive way to process information. Each has special skills.

Left Hemisphere   **Right Hemisphere**

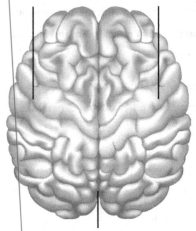

Reticular Activating System

Fulgent Cadences

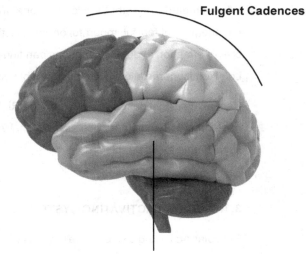

Limbic System

1. LEFT HEMISPHERE

The LEFT HEMISPHERE of your brain includes these important functions.

Your ability to:

> **Solve problems**
> **Concentrate**
> **Read words in sequence**
> **Remember patterns**
> **Perform routine activities**

The calculating, communicative and strategy-oriented Left Hemisphere can be influenced by elements in the environment. Hard-wired for certain skills, the left brain is logical, precise and respects the concept of time.

2. RIGHT HEMISPHERE

The RIGHT HEMISPHERE of your brain also performs many important functions.

These include your ability to:

> **Distinguish letters and pictures**
> **Interpret non-verbal information**
> **Gather input that is new and novel**
> **Attend to body signals**
> **Understand spatial relationships**

When studied, the right brain's emotional focus has been linked to the avoidance or the engagement of fearful, mournful or pessimistic attitudes. When coupled with the strategic left brain's attention to details, emotions can find peace. The harmonious marriage of the Right and Left Hemispheres allows you to know what you want ... and why.

Recent investigations uncovered that the Right Hemisphere's insular cortex holds the files for goal-directed behavior as well as intuition. When you are exploring parts of your brain, take special time to locate this area.

3. RETICULAR ACTIVATING SYSTEM

Reticular Activating System is responsible for these as well as many other functions:

Sorting incoming information

Synthesizing cognition

Regulating the transition between sleep and wakefulness

Coordinating perceptions for accurate responses and expressions

Survival instincts

In the midbrain, a group of nuclei at the top of the brain stem make up your Reticular Activating System. When triggered they release neurotransmitters that set neurons firing throughout the brain to focus and sort incoming information.

4. LIMBIC SYSTEM

The Limbic System is where the most basic cerebral reactions are generated. The Limbic System is a set of brain structures located in the pre- and sub-cortex. Your desires and urges, as well as survival directives are processed here. The main modules of this system include these important components. The thalamus acts as a relay station and directs incoming information to the appropriate parts of the brain for processing. The hypothalamus (in conjunction with the pituitary gland) adjusts the body to keep it optimally adapted to the environment. The hippocampus (named after a seahorse and looking like a gentle paw) is fundamental in laying down long-term memories. The amygdala, located in front of the hippocampus is the place where fear is generated and registered.

For reference, here are five functions of the Limbic System.

Emotional responses

Coding experiences to prioritize actions

Pleasure and sustained feelings of well-being

Long-term storage of memories about emotional decisions

Empathetic responses

All incoming sensory information (except smell) first goes to the central part of the Limbic System that acts as a relay station for other parts of the brain. Smells that are pleasant go to the frontal lobes of the Right Hemisphere of the brain. Unpleasant odors activate the amygdala in the Limbic System as well as the cortex in the temporal lobe of the Right Hemisphere. This is significant, for many intuitives can pick up multiple layers of information from odors.

5. FULGENT CADENCES

Named by the author for their bright and rhythmic emenations, Fulgent Cadences, are non-physical components of the brain's magnetic field that file and transfer vital information.

Fulgent Cadences are energetic frequencies that look like concentric halos that support your:

Decision-making processes

Effective intuition

Action-motivated will

Growth and development

Choices that foster evolutionary and constructive attitudes

Stimulating sections of the Fulgent Cadences that are located at the temporal lobe can produce feelings of spiritual transcendence. This area is not to be confused with the area around the right frontal insular cortex that activates goal-directed behavior as well as intuitional insight.

You can design a personal access and retrieval system to manage all five parts of your brain. This is based on your ability to localize these areas by bringing focused attention to them. For example, if your conscious mind is interested in accessing the quality of your clairaudience or clairvoyance, it can scan through the other systems to find consistent vibratory patterns.

Many readers are acquainted with the use of kinesiological muscle testing. This feedback technique can be used as a verification tool to monitor your explorations of the energetic parts of your brain.

Exercise #1

Study an illustration of the five areas of the brain. Imagine that you can become tiny enough to easily explore inside each one and then return to your full body size.

1. Bring your attention to the Left Hemisphere of your brain. Experience your own inner geography.

2. Now, move your attention to the Right Hemisphere of your brain. Lightly explore. While there you may discover your right frontal insular cortex.

3. Focus your attention on the Reticular Activating System. This is the area where incoming information is encoded to its relevancy. Widen your awareness of both sensory and meta-sensory data by allowing it to enter and be filed.

4. Move your attention to the area that houses emotions. This is called the Limbic System. The wisdom of your system can help you find the components of this important area. Breathe normally.

Exercise #2

After your initial investigation, delve deeper by using the prompts from the Sensory Awareness Lists to assist your continued exploration. What conscious responses did you get, if any, from each area of your brain?

Sensory Awareness List

> **Surface/ internal texture**
> **Temperature**
> **Density**
> **Solidity**
> **Substance**
> **Sensory associations**

Exercise #3

Close your eyes and begin your exploration at the base of your skull. Slowly move your attention away from your physical body to the electromagnetic field that surrounds your head. Move your attention up and around your body to sense the energies. Perhaps, with relaxed attention, you will be able to identify energetic sensations prompted by the following Awareness List.

Colors

Light and shadow

Movement

Sizes and relative dimensions

Shapes

Rhythmic sound

Dull noise

Sharp resonance

High or low in pitch

Surface/ internal texture

Temperature

Density

Solidity

Substance

When you have finished exploring your Fulgent Cadences, stretch and touch your toes.

Exercise #4

Visit a gift shop or the housewares section of a department store. Choose an item on display to use for this exercise.

Without touching the item, move your attention to the brain areas that help you gather information. Focus on the powers you have in your:

Reticular Activating System

Limbic System

Fulgent Cadences

Right Hemisphere of your brain

Left Hemisphere of your brain

What impressions did you receive?

If you didn't access any particular information, do not be disturbed.

In time you may receive images, feelings, or even hear thoughts or words.

Jot down all impressions you receive. This supports your experience.

Exercise #5

Ask a colleague to provide you with a man-made object that he/she knows about. The item could be a family heirloom or something rather new. Sit quietly. With your eyes closed mentally refer to the categories on the Sensory Awareness List to ascertain accurate insights about the object. Open your eyes and jot these down impressions that came into your mind. When you feel you have completed the exercise, share your insights with your colleague to gain deeper understanding of the information you have received.

If you did not get any information, do not be disturbed.

NOTES

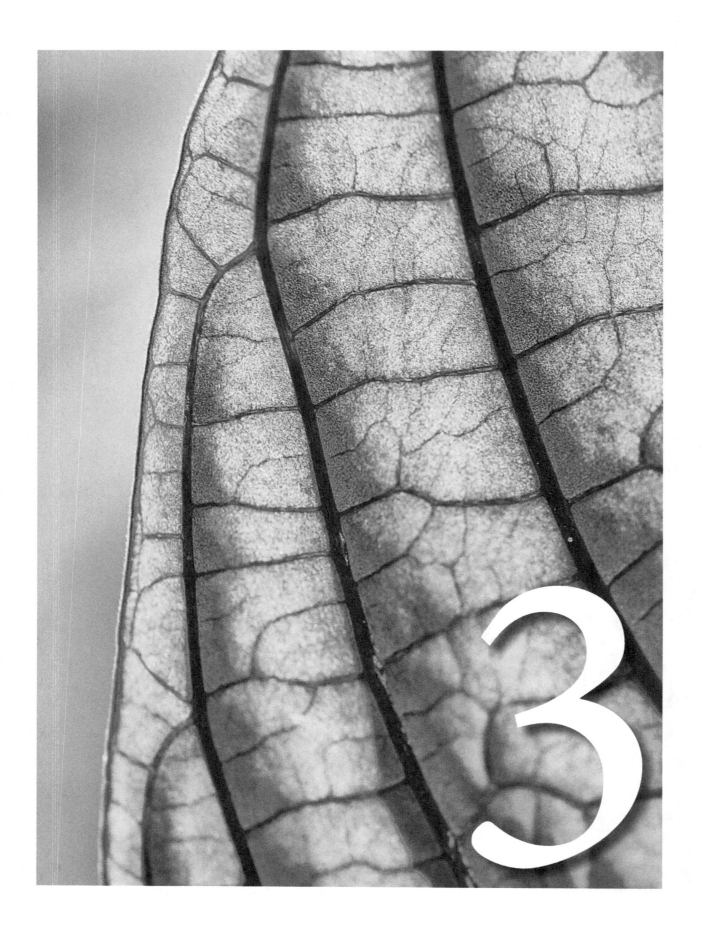

3

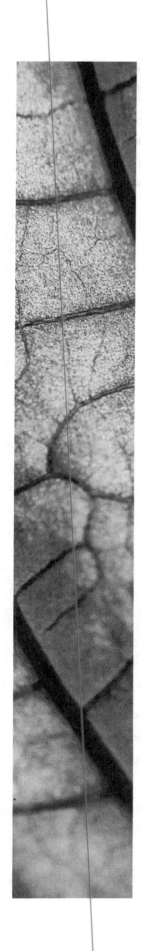

CHAPTER 3
CERTAINTY AND TRUST

In this chapter your goals are to attain a trust and a feeling of certainty about the intuitional information you receive. Discover ways to differentiate your intuitive insights from logical deductions and your emotional reactions.

Your confidence as an intuitive increases when you can recognize three distinctive types of vibrations. The first vibrations are feelings associated with your intuition. The second are your emotional responses and the ambient associations. The third are deductive reasoning's conclusions.

Your Pillar of Intuition is:

> **Patient**
>
> **Wise**
>
> **Appreciative**
>
> **Supportive**
>
> **Available to you at all times**

Information that comes to you from your intuition with sensory details does not upset your mind or make it feel stressed in any way.

Your Emotional Nature is:

> **Connected to your body-rooted survival mechanisms**
>
> **Empathetic**
>
> **Mood-related**
>
> **Includes such automatic responses as: disgust, fear,**
>> **anger, and parental love**
>
> **Instrumental in creating short and long- term memories**

Your Deductive Reasoning's Conclusions are:

> **Triggered by recollection and imagining**
>
> **Included in your self-awareness and your reflections**
>
> **Processed with intellectual insights**
>
> **Responded with Emotional and Deductive Reasoning**

Practice the following exercises to sharpen your awareness of the differences between pure intuitive information, defense mechanism reactions and deductive reasoning. Use the Sensory List to help you differentiate emotional reactions, empathy, intellectual processing and accurate intuitional insight.

Imagine that a friend of yours told you that she discovered that her favorite necklace was missing after house guests stayed at her beautiful home for the weekend. She named four suspects and told you about each of their characters.

She asked you to give her feedback.

a) Eager to help your friend feel less upset, you offer a determination based on listening to the backgrounds of the people who stayed there. Although you have never met any of them, you have concluded that one was most likely guilty because there was a motive and time enough for the suspect to accomplish the deed. (You were using deductive reasoning.)

b) Eager to help your friend feel less upset, you asked about each suspect's feelings toward your friend and their interest in the necklace. Then you subjectively reviewed each one's relationship with the others. You gave her your opinion. (You were using emotional response judgment.)

c) Eager to help your friend feel less upset, you asked her to recount anything that came to her mind about the weekend. As she spoke, rather than evoking pictures from her words, you allowed your Sensory File List to provide you with ambient and specific information using your non-judgmental and non-emotional intuition. (You provided the space to allow insights to emerge.)

Exercise #1

Person A and Person B sit across from each other in two chairs.

Person B listens to a story that Person A tells from his own life about something that was problematic and then solved. Without letting Person B know the ending, Person A tells the story and before explaining the outcome, allows Person B to find his deductive, emotional and intuitive reactions.

Person A will help Person B with details received to confirm intuitional insights.

To test your progress while practicing this exercise, ask about any details you found when in the role of Person B.

Person A and Person B switch roles and continue the exercise.

CONTINUED STUDY

During the week, listen to the stories others share with you. As they speak, listen in three distinct ways:

a. from an empathetic perspective - to feel their emotions

b. to understand their perceptions, their powers of observation and thinking patterns

c. from an intuitive attitude that allows you to access images, sensations and auditory input as a you hear about an event

Exercise #2

Imagine that you have been invited to dinner at a restaurant in a city far from your home. Because you have no knowledge about the place, you ask about it.

Person A describes a restaurant that he actually knows. Then Person B asks questions about the place. These will naturally give Person B a chance to use his emotional responses, deductive reasoning and intuition.

Person B shares with Person A in what ways he used each of these. Any intuitive insights can be confirmed at this time.

Repeat this exercise by finding other places at distance that Person A wants to talk about. Person B can use these as a destination to gain insight.

Person A and B can switch roles and continue.

Exercise #3

Read a magazine article and as you respond to the paragraphs, notice if your mind is reflecting on emotional, deductive reasoning responses or if you receive intuitive information from the words.

Exercise #4

Listen to the radio and discern if the music played is a recording that is more than ten years old, more than 20 years old, or older. Find out this answer by first using your intuition, and then try using your deductive reasoning. Lastly exercise your emotional responses to gain your correct answer.

Exercise #5

Pick up a book. Without opening the cover, can you tell the age of the book? Find out the answer by first using your intuition, and then your deductive reasoning and lastly through emotional responses. When you have chosen one date that all three agree upon, open the book to the copyright page to test your accuracy.

Practice an attitude of certainty and trust when you call upon your intuition for insight.

NOTES

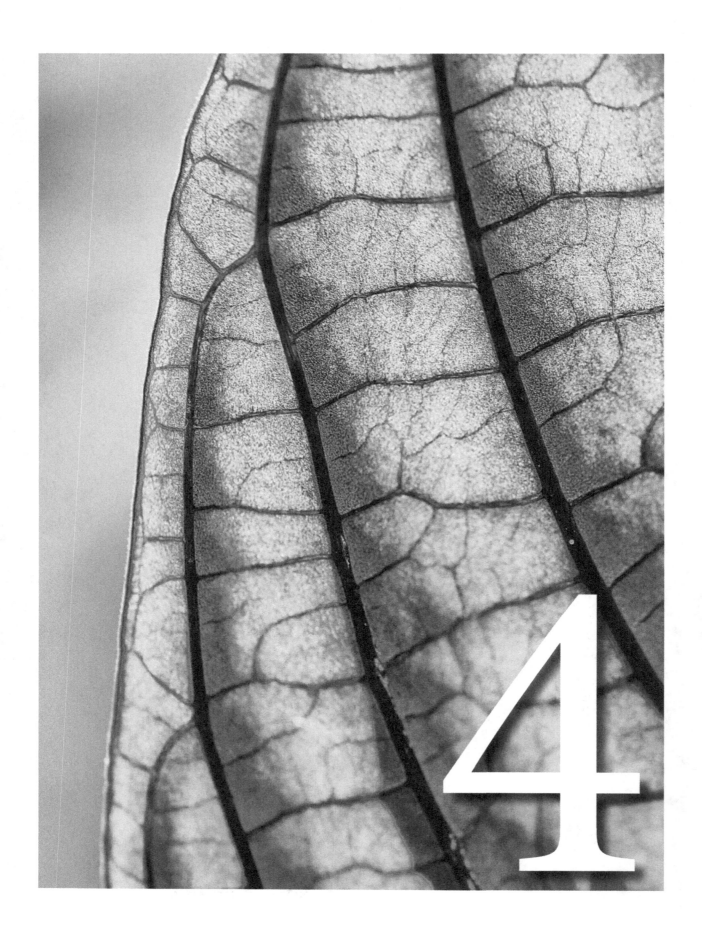

4

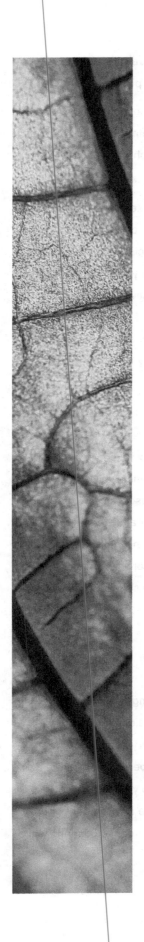

CHAPTER 4
RIBBONS OF REALITY

The goal of this chapter is to weave your sensory, deductive, intuitive and energetic consciousnesses into a rational problem-solving tool to widen your present reality.

Imagine that your perceptions and awarenesses generate separate strings of continuously coded data. Seamlessly, your sensations, feelings, responses, intuitions and electromagnetic field's impressions interweave to what we will call your ribbons of reality. Each strand contributes important perspectives to your problem-solving skills.

To support your ongoing enhancement process, continue focusing on the pleasures available to your five senses. Practice listening to your thoughts. Follow your reasoning processes. Notice if you are distracted easily by visual or auditory input. Do you use mental discipline to return to the same thought after a distraction? Your reasoning mind's ribbon is fairly easy to track. With a bit of practice, you can follow the intuitive strand that is completely free of deductive reasoning. This is your intuition. The intuition string has a distinct quality. It is a string of ongoing clarity free of opinions and emotional overlays. You will be able to discern your intuition through its dissimilarities to other faculties. The more you sense how your reality ribbons are woven, the more you can manage them to serve your purposes.

Exercise # 1

Find a place where you can sit alone in pleasant surroundings. In this exercise you will eat a sandwich. Follow your thoughts and actions as an observer of your experience while eating half the sandwich in a customary manner. Eat the other half by creating a sensory-filled experience using your Sensory Focus List. If you receive intuitive flashes, incorporate these into your experience by knowing that you did not use your reasoning process to get the information. Engage all the ribbons of reality in this exercise by allowing them to come to your conscious mind. As with sensory experiences practice finding reasoning and intuition ribbons in the specific and ambient parts of your consciousness.

Exercise #2

Return to the place where you practiced Exercise #1. Sense the surroundings and eat another sandwich. For this exercise, slow down the eating process. Chew your food carefully. Do not let your mind wander to any thoughts of the past or future. Enjoy the sensory aspects of the present. While you are open to the sensory information, notice if you begin to pick up meta-sensory information too. If so, incorporate these intuitive insights into your experience. Take note of any information – beyond your knowing – that relates to the environment or the sandwich. Let the ribbons of reality bring the intuitive information to your consciousness while relaxed and enjoying the sensory world.

Exercise #3

In this exercise you will ask two colleagues to each make you one cup of tea. Both cups will be served to you on a tray. You will pick up Cup A and take a drink. Then you will pick up Cup B and take a drink. From the experience of touching the cup, and using your reality ribbons, can you identify who prepared which cup of tea for you?

Now ask each of the colleagues to put thought-forms about a particular type of dessert into another cup of tea that they prepare for you. Can you identify who made the cup of tea and what was the thought-formed dessert?

Exercise #4

Person A and Person B are a distance apart and are in contact with each other by telephone or Skype. Person A asks Person B to look at a sheet of colored paper that is one of the colors of the rainbow. Person B sends the color using his conscious mind. Person A receives it and Person B verifies that the color is accurate. Once this is done easily, test how many of the elements of the Sensory File List that Person A can access about Person B's environment at distance.

Exercise #5

Person A finds two of his cotton shirts and asks Person B to iron the first one. While ironing it, Person B will think about how tired Person A will feel when he wears the shirt. Then Person B irons the second shirt and thinks about how energized, refreshed and uplifted Person A will feel wearing the second shirt. Person A wears each shirt for 10 minutes. He then recounts his physical reactions to the experiment of wearing the emotionally programmed clothing.

NOTES

NOTES

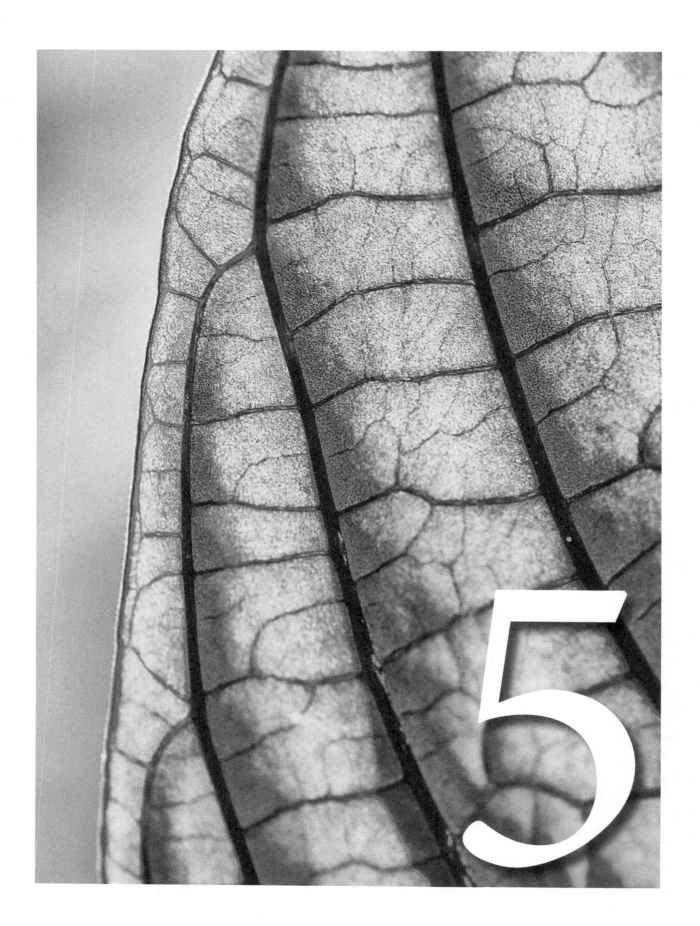

5

CHAPTER 5
FIVE FINGER FLICK —
A TECHNIQUE

In this chapter you will awaken ancient knowledge hidden in each of your fingers.

Follow these instructions and build an energetic program using your own hand. After researching this technique, those who studied it found that this seemingly simple process designed by the author can support your:

Awareness

Flexibility

Concentration

Reaction time

Sense of direction

Mental visualization

Adaptation within new situations

Spontaneous insights to aid problem solving

Error detection

Poise of movement

The Buddhists call the use of hand placement in certain positions - Quiet Hands. Over centuries it has been explained that there are connecting points in the nervous system that become activated when you align your hands in these prearranged ways. Activated nerve circuits stimulate specific mind-body functions. These are called Nadis. In combination with routine health practices, this sequence of hand placements can help you achieve inner balance if you are feeling vulnerable in crowds or before sleeping at night. Each hand configuration is designed to also help you to protect yourself against those who may be disturbing your inner alignment.

Each finger holds traditional attributes that have been utilized through history in many cultures. Because of their extensive use, these finger alignments have become part of the collective consciousness. You can utilize the latent power in your own hands by programming your fingers to enhance your intuition. When you desire to strengthen or recalibrate your intuition's operating system, your five fingers can help you.

PART ONE

This energetic technique has two parts. You only have to do this first part once to set the outline into your system. Then, when you feel you would like to balance yourself, run the balancing program using the simple set of movements explained in Part Two.

To Program Your System:

1. Touch your thumb and your little finger together. You can choose to use either hand. As you do so, you restore the connection to precision and the inner subtle communication that stabilizes and supports your pillar of intuition. Touching your thumb and little finger organizes the two hemispheres of your brain and your Limbic System.

Release the connection of the two fingers. Proceed to Step 2.

2. Touch your thumb and your fourth finger together. As you do so you are bringing vital healthy self-assertion to your emotions. This enhances your clarity and stamina. This step connects you to the Source of Truth so that accurate information can be funneled to your intuition.

Release the connection of the two fingers. Proceed to Step 3.

3. Touch your thumb and middle finger together. This connection enforces the conscientiousness to take on the tasks of decision-making with action, security, initiative and efficiency.

Release the connection of the two fingers. Proceed to Step 4.

4. Touch your thumb and your index finger together. Your pillar of Intuition and your relationship to the Ruler of all Nature are amplified with this connection. Programming this action into the sequence integrates your inner wisdom to accomplish your problem- solving goals with integrity and competence. Proceed to Step 5.

5. Close your hand into a gentle fist with your thumb facing the sky.

Lower your head so that your chin rests near your chest.
Exhale while resting your chin closer to your chest.
Stretch your head upward as you inhale.
Rest your thumb on the knuckle of your index finger.
Blink. This signals the end of the programming.

PART TWO

When you feel you want to run this valuable energetic program, follow these simple steps.

1. Using the thumb of either hand, slide your nail along the tip of each finger beginning with the little finger. This action should be done with the amount of pressure that produces a slight lightening of the color of the skin.

2. After sliding your thumbnail over the fingertips of the other four fingers on the same hand, lower

your head so that your chin rests near your chest. Exhale and relax your chin closer to your chest. Stretch your head upward as you inhale. Continue to breathe as you fold your thumb down over the first joint of your index finger. Blink.

End of the process.

Please use this energetic program less than four times in a day.

BONUS EXERCISES

The goal of these bonus exercises is to help you interpret impulses of sensory data, body signals, feelings, and flashes of sequential intuitive information.

Remember, that when assessing intuitive data, do not edit, embellish, or fill in missing pieces with deductive reasoning bridges. Maintain your composure. If you lose your place due to overstimulation of input, then stop. Relax. Center yourself. Begin where you left off or find another intuitive landmark and continue.

Exercise #1

Person A - places a fist-sized object in the center of a piece of typing paper and draws a circle around the object with a bold black marker. He leaves the room.

Person B removes the object from the circle when he pleases.

Person A, not able to see if the object is in the circle or not, practices differentiating when there is an object in the circle or when it is empty by calling out when it is taken away or is replaced.

Certainty and trust increase as one can differentiate feelings from this subtle vibrational exercise.

Exercise #2

Person A places six objects on a tray. He shows them to Person B. After 30 seconds:
Person A places a towel over the objects.
Person B writes down the six objects and includes as many details as he can remember.

When Person B has finished writing, Person A shows Persona B the tray's object to validate his written answers.

Person A out of sight of Person B then takes one of the six objects and places it alone on the tray. Again he covers the tray with a towel.

Person B uses intuition to sense which of the six objects is hidden.

After Person A removes the towel to reveal the object, Person B recounts the reasons he chose the object.

Exercise #3

Person A places six objects on a tray. Minutes before showing the tray to Person B, Person A chooses one of the six objects, spins it on the table and replaces it on the tray out of sight of Person B.

Person B looks at the objects and quickly discerns which of the six has been recently gyrated. He then explains the reasons for his choice.

Exercise #4

Person A places two coins on a tray. Person B watches as Person A who has instilled tender or other pleasant emotional thoughts into a third coin, places Coin 3 near the other coins. Person B notes his emotional responses to the introduction of the third coin.

Repeat this experiment. Person A replaces the third coin with a coin that has been instilled with non-pleasant emotional thought-forms. Person B explains his reactions to the introduction of this coin.

Person A neutralizes the thought-forms from the coins and asks if Person B senses anything from either of the third coins.

Exercise #5

Person A closes his eyes, thinks of a fruit or vegetable and holds out his hands to Person B.

Person B clasps hands with Person A. Then he closes his eyes and uses his powers of intuition to receive the information of the fruit or vegetable that was telepathically sent.

In 1971 a telepathic experiment was conducted during the Apollo 14 mission. While in space, Astronaut Edgar D. Mitchell concentrated on a sequence of 25 numbers. This he repeated 200 times. Two of the four recipients on earth received 51 correct answers. The law of averages would have been below 40. It is well known that telepathy transcends time. This is one of the few recorded experiments that also includes the stretch of 150,000 miles of space between the sender and receiver.

BONUS SUGGESTIONS

Eat moderately and avoid processed foods with refined ingredients that have traveled long distances to get to your table. Additives and preservatives may cause you to minimize your intuitive skills. The more sensitive you become the more you may feel uncomfortable if you take on vibrations aligned with the food you eat.

Get to know growers who support community gardening and farming endeavors. Consider creating your own Diamond Garden. Utilize the available resources that include energetic assistance to grow your garden.

If you eat fish, avoid shellfish, cod and others that hold high levels of contaminants and heavy metals. Minimize salt and sugar. Learn to identify the smell and taste of the ingredients you eat. If you get an intuitive feeling not to eat something - don't eat it!

Avoid chemicals for cleaning your environment and body. Use natural products such as low-phosphate and unscented soaps, baking soda, borax and vinegar. Avoid any product that causes your body to go into defense.

Take regular breaks if you spend much time in front of a computer. Notice how you feel after using a mobile phone. Learn what experience causes changes in your intuition, your deductive reasoning, your emotions and your memory. Discipline yourself to experience new things. Remain interested in the elements of your world. Design the information you receive from your senses into a coordinated and systematized filing activity of pleasure and beauty. Practice sharpening your short and long-term memory.

Drink water. Remember that nutrients that are commonly depleted in active adults include vitamin A, E and C as well as the B vitamins and the minerals zinc, selenium, calcium, magnesium, iron, potassium and sulfur. When engaged in the extended use of your intuition, your body utilizes many carbohydrates, proteins and fats.

Potassium, calcium and magnesium help your system assimilate incoming information. Potassium is essential for most physiologic activities. Calcium and magnesium are vital in supporting the functioning of the nerves and also your immune system's functions.

Restful sleep will aid your evolutionary process. Practice remembering your dreams.

NOTES

ABOUT THE AUTHOR

Ms. Gurnee is known as a world-wide resource for practitioners and alternative health enthusiasts. Since childhood she has identified energetic information contained in the electromagnetic fields around people and animals. Her skill in reading vibrations and teaching the language of energetics has directed her path for the last decade to teach advanced observational skills to doctors, dentists and health care professionals in Switzerland, Germany, Austria, and the United States.

When not traveling Ms. Gurnee offers private health consultations by phone. For more information about her upcoming schedule visit *www.suegurnee.com*.

She is the founder of, and currently acting director of Fields of Understanding School of Principled Consciousness. For more information about this innovative borderless classroom school visit *www.fieldsofunderstanding.com*.

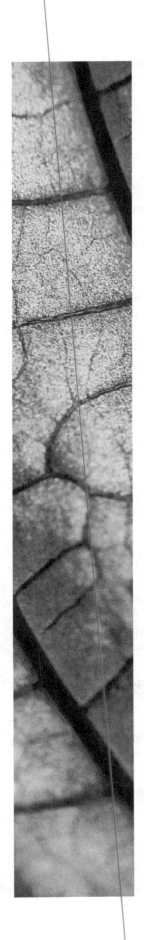

GLOSSARY

Association – a learned correlation between two actions or elements often referred to when dealing with stimuli and response.

Chakra – from Sanskrit for wheel – a whirling vortex of energy and association of energy with physical and mental functions with fulgent cadences

Clairaudience – the ability to hear things nor perceived with five senses.

Clairvoyance – the ability to see objects and events beyond proximinal space and time.

Cognitive theory – how the mind processes information with focus on reasoning, memory and problem solving.

Collective consciousness – the part of ourselves that registers the energies of the combined feelings, thoughts and sensations shared by all humans.

Defense mechanisms – ways humans protect against imagined pain or harm. These include – denial, intellectualization, projection, rationalization, regression, repression and masking.

Diamond Gardening – visit www.diamondgardening.org

Empathy – the awareness and understanding of others' feelings.

Fulgent Cadences – fulgent - bright and shimmery – cadences – rhythms – electromagnetic emanations around the brain that replenish and assist problem-solving and decision-making.

Innate – characteristics inherent in an organism.

Intellectual processing is a general term for rational thinking, problem solving, inductive and deductive reasoning and intuition.

Intuitional insight – problem-solving process that targets information about a person, place, or thing in the past, present or future using subliminal states of awareness beyond rational thinking. Using inner attention management skills, impulses are accessed for accurate information retrieval.

The Limbic System, as the seat of emotions, it gathers the emotional components involved with sensory input.

Meta-sensory – pertaining to awareness beyond the confines of the mechanics of sensory awareness.

Mudras – symbolic hand gestures used through history to stimulate different parts of the body and associated energetic pathways.

Nadis – pathways through which subtle energy moves from the chakras to all parts of the body.

Perception – the process of organizing and creating meaning to sensations received.

Problem-solving uses the impulses from intellectual and intuitional thinking from which to figure a solution. Errors in the functionality of one's internal Reticular Activating System or Limbic System will affect the quality of rational thinking. Errors in intellectual functioning can also alter the clarity of intuitional accuracy. Errors in problem-solving can be caused by inner contradictions, false conclusions, erroneous beliefs and misunderstandings.

Rational thinking is a process that uses reasoning powers. Moral and ethical foundations, logical guidelines and codes of behavior create integrity-laden conclusions that structure the reasoning functions of rational thinking.

The Reticular Activating System stimulates neuron circuits to coordinate and file incoming stimuli from the five senses.

Right Frontal Insular Cortex is a component of the Limbic System, it responds to emotional input and synthesizes subjective emotional experiences. It helps map the visceral states and brings emotions from the Limbic System to conscious feelings.

NOTES

NOTES

NOTES

NOTES

Printed in the United States
By Bookmasters

Printed in the United States
By Bookmasters